Real People...Real

M000267270

A New Normal

Learning to Live with Grief and Loss

Second Edition

Darlene F. Cross, MS, LMFT

Darlene F. Cross, M.S., M.F.T., Inc.
Las Vegas, Nevada

A New Normal: Learning to Live with Grief and Loss
Second Edition

Published by Darlene F. Cross, M.S., M.F.T., Inc.
www.darlenecross.com

ISBN 978-0-9843441-7-8

Book and cover design and layout by Robert Goodman, Silvercat™, Encinitas, California

printed in the United States of America

With deepest gratitude and appreciation for Gary Gardia,
my mentor and colleague in the world of grief and loss
work, my relentless muse in writing my books,
and the dear friend I can always count on to be there.

And with unconditional love and gratitude for
the two greatest teachers I have ever had, my sons,
Jason and Brandon Cross.

From *Fire in the Belly: On Being a Man,* by Sam Keen

You may be certain that if you want to be a pilgrim, you are
going to get lost. The old Boy Scout manual offered some practical wisdom for those who are lost on any quest. First, don't
panic. Second, stop doing what you were doing. Third, sit down
and calm yourself. Fourth, look for landmarks. Fifth, follow
trails or streams that lead downhill or toward open space. A
mountain man was once asked if he often got lost. "No," he
replied. "I've never been lost. But sometimes for a month or
two I didn't know how to get where I was going."

Contents

2017 Introduction 11

2010 Introduction 13

Chapter 1: Making the Grief Process Work for You 15

Am I Normal?. 15

Ann's Story—Did Ann Fail Her Loved One? 16

  My Comments to Ann 17

Stages, Formulas, and Blueprints! Beware! 17

Grief—Friend or Foe? 19

New Normal Tips 19

No Short Cuts. 19

Tom's Story—Did Tom Get a Free Pass?. 19

Yes to Emotions, Yes to Life. .20

Chapter 2: Good-Bye to Your Old Normal 21

Letting Go of What? 21

A Death-Dying Culture 22

You Aren't Sick 22

Pauline's Story—Grief Found Pauline at the Grocery Store 23

I Wasn't Prepared for That! 23

A Year of Firsts 24

New Normal Tips 24

The Gift of Clarity. 25

What Do I Do?. 25

The Power of Rituals 27

Margie and the Ashes 27

Chapter 3: Impact from Types of Loss 29

The First of Two Evils—Anticipated Loss 29

Amy's Story—A Few Words Can Mean So Much 30

  My Comments on Amy's Story 30

Bumps in the Road 31

Mary's Story—No Good Deed Goes Unpunished 31

  My Comments to Mary—Trading Guilt for Peace of Mind 31

  The Conclusion of Mary's Story. 32

Pro-Active Grief Is a Thief 32

The "D" Word. 33

What Do I Do when Someone I Love Is Dying? 33

The Other Evil—Sudden Loss. .34

Reactive Grief. 34

What Do I Do after a Sudden Loss? 34

Death by Internet 35

You Have Mail—Rose's Story. .35

"What If" Game 37

Chapter 4: Loss by Type of Relationship 39

Parent Loss. 39

  Young Child Loss of Parent. .39

Alice's Story—The Dangers of Magical Thinking. 40

  Older Child Loss of Parent. .41

Nikki's Story—Lost in Time 41

  Teen Loss of Parent 42

  Adult Loss of Parent. 43

Spouse or Partner Loss. 43

Harry's Story—Invalid and Invisible 44

Sibling Loss. 45

Friend Loss. 46

Pet Loss—A Silence So Loud. .46

What Do I Do?. 47

Chapter 5: Detours on the Way to a New Normal 49
I Quit. 49
It's Raining Losses 49
Secondary Losses Are Sneaky! 50
New Normal Tips 51
What Do Dirty Laundry and Unresolved Grief Have
in Common? 51
Steve's Story—The Cowboy and the Baby Chick 52
Closure Confusion 52
Chris' Story—Closure Is in the Eye of the Beholder. 53
Road Blocks to a New Normal—Lawsuits 54
A Giant Step to a New Normal—Funerals. 55
Bereavement Groups 55

Chapter 6: Significant Others 57
Divorce Losses 57
Loss of Best Friend. 58
Loss of Trust 58
Loss of Hope 58
Loss of Privacy. 58
Loss of an Intact Family 59
Reversing Significant 60
What Do I Do?. 60

Chapter 7: Other Losses 63
Loss of Financial Well Being. 63
Loss of Job. 64
New Normal Tips 64
Loss of Career 64
New Normal Tips 64
Loss of Business 64
New Normal Tips 65

New Normal Tips *66*
  Work Now, Feel Later *66*
Loss through Aging *67*
Loss of Health *68*
I Surrender *69*
What Do I DO? *69*

Chapter 8: Questions Answered and Myths Dispelled 71

Chapter 9: Helplessness to Resilience—The Author's Story . .81
The Background *81*
From Helplessness *83*
To Resilience *87*

Conclusion 89

2017 Introduction

I had no idea what I was doing when I started writing *A New Normal: Learning to Live with Grief and Loss* eight years ago. Had it not been for the encouragement of friends and colleagues, the book wouldn't even exist. I did my best at the time but honestly never imagined anyone would buy it, let alone care to read what I had written. I had no idea how wrong I was.

The simple little book traveled far and wide, taking on a life of its own. Every person I met along the way, every direct or indirect piece of feedback I received, every new experience and awareness I had motivated me to want to write a new and better version.

I have listened carefully to all of you, including the people who like the book and people who don't. You were whispering in my ear as I wrote this Second Edition. I heard how you resonated with the case studies and stories and I added more. Many sections have been expanded and some completely rewritten. I was surprised at how strongly many of you connected with the section comparing divorce to death, so I expanded that into an entire chapter on this subject alone. I also like to believe I have become a better writer over the years, a more skilled clinician as I celebrate 20 years, and a wiser woman in my own relentless pursuit of personal growth and development.

To all of you who have supported me in my work, I am eternally grateful. I appreciate your kindness in seeing past the less-than-perfect efforts of a new writer, looking deeper to find the messages inside. If you are new to my books, you will meet a more seasoned writer and see a more polished publication, but hopefully the messages remain the same. After all, it was always about the messages.

2010 Introduction

Have you experienced the profound loss of someone dear to you? Are you feeling helpless, numb, overwhelmed, maybe disoriented as if nothing around you makes sense anymore? You may even be embarrassed you are so emotional, or not emotional enough. Or maybe you are like I was, struggling to gain a foothold after my own first significant loss when I didn't know which way to turn first.

I knew I wasn't the first or the only person to experience the unexpected death of someone so dear, but that's exactly how it felt. The questions I had then are the same questions people have been bringing into my therapy practice now for two decades. People from all walks of life with all types of losses have the same questions and the same need for information.

That's why I wrote *A New Normal*. You have likely found books of inspiration, books offering quick and easy solutions when what you need are respectful and practical answers. You want information that helps you make sense out of what you are thinking, feeling and experiencing. You want a book that helps you know what to DO.

Inside *A New Normal*, you'll discover how to understand what is happening to you, where you are in your grief process, and what you can expect as you go forward. You will learn that it is okay to give yourself permission to grieve, that grieving is part of being human, and that while grief is universal each loss is unique.

You will meet other newly bereaved people in *A New Normal*, including some interesting characters that will prove that yes, you can still laugh! You will gain tips and learn practical and proven ways to navigate through your grief and your loss. Once you understand how grief works, the process may be a little less painful and a lot more productive.

I never had any ambition to write a book. This book gave me no choice, it demanded to be written. It is the book I never found when I needed it most. It is the book I want my loved ones to have when the day comes they need it most. If the insights and stories you are about to read help you understand one thing you didn't understand before about your loss, if your pain is lightened even the slightest, then this book will be a success.

You've waited long enough in this place where every minute is an eternity. It's time to take back your life, time to work with your grief in a way that honors both you and your loved one. Let's get started.

NOTE: All stories in this book are based on actual cases, some stories volunteered by friends of the author, and some from the author herself. All names and some details have been changed or multiple cases condensed into one to protect the identity and confidentiality of the people involved.

Chapter 1

Making the Grief Process Work for You

Does it seem impossible you could ever make sense of the chaos you are experiencing after the death of your loved one? Have you heard advice you question? Have you read materials that left you with more questions than you had before?

In this chapter you will learn how to recognize what is happening to you. You will gain knowledge that will begin to make some sense from the senseless, giving you a greater feeling of power in a powerless situation. And, you will see how grieving after a loss is a very normal human experience none of us gets to escape.

Am I Normal?

If you are feeling confused and disoriented after your loss, then you are right on track. Even your body may feel like it no longer belongs to you, and your mind has temporarily left the building. While these feelings would be troubling in your everyday life, they are completely normal when you have experienced a significant loss.

The human reaction to witnessing or learning of the death of a loved one is shock. Your mind fights to grasp some semblance of reality, at the same time rejecting the reality that has completely and irreversibly changed your life and your world from one moment to the next.

As normal as experiencing shock may be, it can interfere at critical moments with your ability to react as you ordinarily would. What could be more disconcerting than to open your mouth and have nothing come out when you are desperate to speak? How frustrating is it to pick up the phone to dial home in an emergency only to find you have forgotten your own number?

Shock is the culprit when everything around you seems to be moving in slow motion. Your body feels like it weighs a thousand pounds as if you are moving through quicksand. Every breath takes effort. Words just don't work the way they should and thoughts race manically. The famous Salvador Dali art that portrays an assortment of drooping, dripping and distorted clocks is a perfect image of this phenomenon and suggests the artist may have known this subject all too well.

Shock is a normal reaction to a very abnormal situation, your body's way of protecting you without a single conscious thought. The slowing down of thoughts and actions are in effect allowing you to process threatening information in a way that is designed to maximize your own chances for survival. Viewed this way, you can see how shock is an incredible coping mechanism, your best friend waiting patiently to help you when you need help most.

Ann's Story—Did Ann Fail Her Loved One?

Ann's husband of over 50 years had an inoperable aneurism. They both knew for years the aneurism could rupture at any time, immediately ending his life, or it might never rupture at all. Advance knowledge did nothing to prepare Ann for the day when "never" ceased to be an option.

The couple was spending a quiet afternoon at home. Ann walked into the next room only to find her husband in the throws of what could only be a ruptured aneurism. She knew she should get help but found herself unable to make even the slightest movement. She stood frozen in horror as the man she loved died right in front of her eyes.

When Ann came to therapy, she explained that she knew there was nothing that she could have done to save her husband's life. She was deeply appreciative of the time she did have with him, more than she had expected. What she was struggling painfully with was the fact she had not acted more quickly at the time, unable to do something as simple as go to the phone and dial 911.

My Comments to Ann

Ann listened intently as I explained to her what was happening to her body physically in this time of crisis and why she had been unable to act. She sat quietly for a few moments, looking down, considering the information. She looked back up at me and she asked, "You mean that was my body keeping me safe?" I assured her that it was. She reached back to pat her own shoulder and with a big smile said, "Thank you, Body!"

Stages, Formulas, and Blueprints! Beware!

You have likely seen many books, models and blueprints about grief that you may or may not be finding helpful. If you come across something that works for you, by all means make the most of it. However, if you come across something that does not work, remember there is no one-size-fits-all solution on how to grieve. It can be frustrating to try to fit into a framework that simply does not suit your needs, match your beliefs or values, possibly creating more obstacles and confusion than you are already experiencing.

The most widely known grief model is commonly referred to as the "Stages of Grief." This theory describes a progression of predictable emotions and how you can expect those emotions to progress. You may be wondering what stage you are in or can expect to soon experience, or if you are even doing it the right way.

It is well known by trained professionals working in the grief community that even the originator of the stages theory later stated regret in having ever introduced the concept that has taken on an identity of its own. What was originally a theory created anecdotally by observing dying patients' emotions and experiences somehow over time morphed into a description of emotions and experiences of people who were grieving a loss—two clearly different groups of individuals.

How could it be that the "Stages of Grief" model could become so widely accepted if it was not built on well researched and validated facts? How is it that the model continues to be frequently recited today by newscasters, talk show participants, comedians, politicians, even some unknowing mental health providers, and more? If the model is questioned, it is not uncommon for some people to react defensively as if the information is sacred and beyond examination or even question.

The early acceptance of the model made sense given that it appeared at a time when there was a void of information to help grief-stricken people who were desperate for answers. What described dying patients over time became accepted as applying equally to the emotions of grieving loved ones left behind. Years later, the theory has been reinforced through endless repetition, frequently tossed out as simple sound bites. It quickly and superficially gives some people the appearance of being experts by commenting on the "Stages of Grief" without doing any of the homework to become real experts.

The truth about grief is it does not come in stages, the process is not linear, and recurring emotions are very much a part of the experience. It is not like a train ride where you check off stations you visit on the way to your destination when your trip finally comes to an end.

Grief comes in cycles, likes waves in the ocean. You can be standing calmly one minute at the water's edge. A wave then comes along that gently rocks you off your balance but you quickly regain your equilibrium; no harm done. Then, you bend over to examine a pretty shell that catches your eye, and just when you least expect it you are knocked over by a wave crashing into your behind and filling your nose with water while you struggle to even catch your breath. That is what grief is really like.

Grief—Friend or Foe?

Grief is a powerful and demanding emotion. It affects you physically, spiritually and emotionally. The indisputable fact is grief will make its demands on you. No one gets a free pass when it comes to the emotions of saying good-bye to someone you love. The choice you do have is whether to work with your grief and allow it to help you through your pain, or resist while your pain patiently follows you around sneaking into unexpected places until it can demand your full and undivided attention.

New Normal Tips

Tip #1: Trust Your Body—If you need to sob, sob for all you're worth and don't care who might hear. If you are okay for the moment and want something to eat because you feel a little hungry, head for the fridge.

Tip #2: Know Emotions Are Fleeting—If you have just destroyed your favorite pillow in a temporary fit of rage and feel a sense of relief, do not be fooled into thinking you are done with anger... or that the rest of your pillows are safe.

Tip #3: Avoid Amateur Experts—If you find yourself the recipient of free advice, keep what works for you and throw the rest away. If you don't want any advice, it's okay to interrupt and change the subject. Remember the only expert on your loss is you.

No Short Cuts

Just as there are no quick or easy steps to an imaginary finish line with grief, there are also no free passes. Some argue that they are fine and do not need to grieve, declaring they just need to get on with their life.

Tom's Story—Did Tom Get a Free Pass?

Tom was an older gentleman attending his first session of a bereavement group for widows and widowers. One participant had just shared a particularly emotional memory that deeply affected everyone in the group—except Tom. He sat stoically throughout the meeting until his silence became awkward and he finally spoke up.

Tom said that he had fought in World War II. He proudly stated soldiers were taught not to feel emotions. Not only could he not allow or process his own emotions over his wife's death, he was nearly crawling out of his skin to even witness the emotions of others. Tom quickly switched the subject to moving on and how he planned to join a singles group to start dating, even though his own loss had been quite recent.

Tom never returned to the group and no one knows what happened to him. What is obvious is that ignoring his emotions did not mean he didn't have them, and no one will ever know the price he paid for holding them inside.

Yes to Emotions, Yes to Life

An argument can be made for getting on with life as usual after experiencing the death of a loved one and not allowing emotions to surface, but at what price? Being turned off to hurtful emotions means you are also turned off to happy emotions. Rejecting emotions is anything but getting on with life, rather it is avoiding it. Emotions come in all shapes and sizes and experiencing the entire range is living life fully, through the good times and the bad and everything in between.

Understanding the cycles of grief means knowing that feelings will come, feelings will go, feelings will change and all are absolutely normal. Your body knows how to grieve, even if your mind does not. Trust your process. Embrace your feelings, knowing some day the hurt will be a little less making a little more room for the joy found in cherished memories.

❧

Now that you realize you can't control or program or escape your grief, are you ready to start working with your grief process? In the next chapter you will learn the skills that will help you say goodbye to your old normal and hello to your new normal.

Chapter 2

Good-Bye to Your Old Normal

Now that you know grief is a process, you may wonder where the process begins. What is the first step to creating your new normal? Your journey starts with what is possibly the toughest task of all, the non-negotiable job of letting go of your old normal.

This chapter will explore what is happening to you in the initial days and weeks following your loss. You will also learn some practical things you can do to help yourself through this difficult time.

Letting Go of What?

Letting go of your old normal is not the same thing as letting go of a person. What does it mean if someone says to you, "You have to let Sam go?" Maybe you aren't ready to let Sam go. Maybe you don't want to let Sam go. Or maybe you don't even believe it's possible to let Sam go because he lives on in your heart and your memories that you don't ever want to let go.

Does this mean you flunk "letting go?" Is it any wonder you are confused about exactly how or if to let go?

Rather than letting go of the person, in this example Sam, what you can let go of is the life you had before Sam died. Your old normal life stopped with Sam's last breath. It is not negotiable; it is not a choice. It is most likely not something you want to do, rather it is something you must do.

The more you resist your new reality, the harder the process will be. The more you accept and allow the process of letting go of your old normal, the more energy you will have to cope with your loss. And the good news is you don't ever have to let go of someone you love, you just keep them in a different place.

A Death-Denying Culture

It doesn't make saying good-bye any easier when we live in a culture that minimizes, denies and sometimes considers death downright inconvenient.

The denial of death is imbedded in our every day language with sayings like, "I could have just died," or "It scared me to death," or "I nearly had a heart attack. You may have surprised yourself when a death-related cliché slipped out of your own mouth after your loss and you froze mid-sentence. We even have a holiday where children dress up as skeletons and zombies.

Then there is the rude and inconsiderate truth that life does go on. Your landlord may express condolences over your loss but still expects the rent check on time. The electric company won't even bother with condolences—pay up or lights out. A generous employer may give you a week off work, but you will be due back the following week ready to resume normal duties.

You Aren't Sick

It seems like every time you turn on the news these days, there is some new report exaggerating facts in favor of theatre. Even simple, every day emotions are often given mental health diagnostic labels, as if there is something pathological about feelings. Grief is simply an emotion, and grieving is the normal reaction to losing someone you love.

The most normal thing in the world is for you to want your life to go back to the way it was before your loss, to turn back the clocks to before they were drooping. You may try to return to your old normal, knowing that the only thing you can go back to is a normal routine. Re-establishing your routine is in fact helpful in coping with your emotions, but should never be confused with believing your grief is finished.

You aren't just saying good-bye to someone you love, rather what you are saying good-bye to is your normal way of living and being. Virtually every area of your life is impacted, starting from the moment you open your eyes in the morning and continuing through to the end of your day. And just as you may be struggling to accept the loss of your old normal, your new normal is already making demands you cannot ignore.

Pauline's Story—Grief Found Pauline at the Grocery Store

It had been only three short weeks since Pauline's husband of over 40 years died. The guests and the mountains of food that came with them were all pretty much gone and it was time to go to the grocery store.

Pauline's routine for many years had been to go to the store every day to choose the freshest ingredients she would use to prepare the evening meal, only this day would prove to be very different. She went into the produce section and was busy picking out the two very best baking potatoes she could find when the shock of her reality hit—she only needed one potato.

Standing there in that moment, Pauline's grief washed over her with an intensity of emotions she had never experienced before. She described being embarrassed to find herself in such a state in public, worried what others must be thinking, yet she was unable to stop her tears.

As Pauline later related her story, using her infallible and priceless sense of humor, she offered a simple solution to her shopping dilemma in the future. "From now on I'm buying potato salad!"

I Wasn't Prepared For That!

You may think it's a strange comparison to consider experiencing your first traumatic loss as kind of like falling in love for the first time, but the two have something very much in common. As a human being, you were born with the capacity for love and the ability to grieve loaded into your hardware, but it seems there's been a serious design flaw because no one loaded the software.

The first time you fall in love and the first time you experience a major loss, you are completely overwhelmed and clueless about how to proceed or what to do with your flood of intense emotions. While falling in love is arguably more enjoyable than grieving, recalling a first broken heart can be an emotionally packed trip down Memory Lane. You do eventually learn how to deal with your emotions, but the first time can be the most challenging.

A Year of Firsts

Most grieving people will tell you the first year is the hardest. It is a year filled with holidays and birthdays experienced for the first time with the ominous absence of the person who died. The first year of grief culminates with what is often the hardest of all, namely the first anniversary of the death. Subsequent years continue to be challenging, but the feelings tend to be less raw, less intense, when they are more familiar.

You muddled through your first love, and your first heartbreak, only to become stronger, more experienced and more resilient. There were likely other heartbreaks along the way, but none that left you as lost as the first. It may be hard to think of grieving as a learned skill, but in many ways that is exactly what it is. It may never get easier, but it does get more familiar.

New Normal Tips

Be Prepared For Special Days—Anticipating upcoming events that may provoke heightened emotions can be the best defense. Maybe you buy your mother's favorite flowers and place them by her picture for Mother's Day. Maybe your Thanksgiving family dinner includes stories of feasts shared in the past when your father was present. Maybe you include his favorite dish in his honor, or maybe you choose to retire it since he isn't there to enjoy it with you. Pretending everything is the same when it is not tends to make special days so much harder when they are already hard enough.

The Gift of Clarity

Life never seems quite as clear as when you view it from the perspective of death. It reminds you that you don't have forever to do the things you want to do. Death can make wasted time and opportunities look foolish and every minute valuable, every relationship precious.

You may find your values shifting. You recognize more easily what is important and discard what is not. You may decide to quit that job where you have been so unhappy for too long. You may decide to terminate an unhealthy relationship. You might even decide to go back to school to get that degree you've always wanted. Creating a new normal isn't easy, it isn't quick, but long-term results can be more than worthwhile. What a beautiful testimony to your loved one's ongoing legacy in your life.

What Do I Do?

- *First, give yourself a break.* You will tend to sleep poorly, dream actively, and disappear into daydreams often. You may find yourself being difficult, short tempered, maybe with no patience for anything or anyone. Maybe you prefer to withdraw into your own private world in the early days following your loss. Maybe you need to surround yourself with people and avoid being alone. Any and all of these behaviors are normal, even typical, for someone who is newly grieving.

  People in pain can easily fail to recognize their own needs. You really can be too physically and emotionally depleted to know what is best for you. To make matters worse, you may have to take on a whole new set of unexpected responsibilities. Maybe you have to cope with a pile of legal paper work you don't understand. You may have to pack up a house that is full of memories, and by a deadline you didn't choose. You might be worried about how you will pay unexpected bills. Is it any wonder you're exhausted?

- *Go with the Flow.* Know that you are going to miss your loved one for the rest of your life. Why wouldn't you? You don't "get over it," you learn to live with it, one minute, one day, one year at a time.

- *Take naps.* If sleeping in your own bed is difficult, try sleeping somewhere else for a few days. Changing routines, even for just a short time, can be helpful when normal routines are too difficult.

- *Assign jobs you need done when people ask what they can do to help.* Give them a task even if it's just to keep them from hovering. Let them do the laundry or wash the dishes or run the vacuum or take care of an errand. If they didn't want to do it, they shouldn't have asked.

- Tell people if you need alone time; tell them if you don't. Don't let others tell you what you need as if they know better than you do. They don't.

- *Journal or write letters to the person who died.* It is okay if what you write is angry or sad; it's okay if it is not. If writing isn't helpful to you, don't write.

- *Let your emotions out.* The more you resist, the harder it gets. Grieving is deeply primal. Don't be afraid to let it look and sound and feel that way. You may want to do this work in private with doors and windows closed so you don't feel the need to monitor your own behavior and to avoid interruptions from worried pets or nosey neighbors.

- *Reject shaming advice* that includes the word "should." You should get over it. You should move on. You should be grateful. Unsolicited advice is not the same as asking for input or an opinion that you want and ask to receive.

- *Be real.* The fact someone else "has it so much worse" may help you put your loss into perspective, but it does not make it any less significant. No two losses are ever exactly the same. Your pain is your pain, and their pain is their pain, and an exact comparison of losses is not even logical let alone possible.

- *Fight the need to DO SOMETHING NOW.* You may be very tempted to sell your house, get cosmetic surgery, or join the Peace Corp. Think twice before making any unnecessary major changes for at least the first few months, and maybe even as much as a year.
- *Be gentle with yourself.* Give yourself time. Know the day will come when you will feel better, but that day just isn't this day.

The Power of Rituals

Rituals can be powerful tools when you are struggling to access or process your emotions, and there is no limit as to what those rituals may be. Group rituals and sharing your pain with others may provide the most healing for you, or you may need to process your emotions in private. Designing your own original rituals that reflect your unique needs can sometimes be the most helpful of all.

Margie and the Ashes

Tera was an accomplished and respected dog expert, the second generation in her European family to breed, train, show and judge internationally. Unfortunately for many, realizing a passion comes with a price and that was more than true for Tera. With the loss of each of her own dogs over the years, from the so-special first to the no-less-special last, Tera had kept each of their ashes in urns lined up on a shelf, cherished memories always close by.

Tired and happy to be returning home after one especially long show tour, nothing could have prepared Tera for what was waiting. She walked in and saw that not only had her house been robbed and vandalized, but all the urns had been knocked to the floor with ashes spilled all over. After the police were gone and Tera was left alone to face the horror of her violated home and life, she knelt to the floor and through tears carefully did her best to collect each precious ash.

The next day at work, Tera told a friend what had happened. She shared that she could no longer bear to keep the ashes with what had happened but wasn't sure what she should do with them. The friend described a beautiful piece of land her family owned on Lake Michigan that included a small cemetery where they scattered all their pets' remains and she encouraged Tera to take her dogs' ashes there as well.

Tera loaded up the car with all the ashes put together in one plastic bag. It seemed fitting she take her two dogs, Margie and Toby, to share in the planned ritual as they each had ancestors amongst the ashes. This was to be a family affair.

Tera arrived at the Lake and was immediately taken by the beauty of the location, comforted that this was certainly the perfect spot for her "little funeral." But, as she prepared to release the ashes, Tera froze, realizing she didn't know what to do next. While she wanted everything to be perfect, all she could remember was being warned about lake-front winds blowing ashes back in the wrong direction.

Help can come in different ways and sometime when you least expect it, and this time it arrived on four feet. Margie knew exactly the right thing to do. She ran over and grabbed the bag of ashes from Tera's hands and ran off with them, shaking her head and the bag back and forth until the bag ruptured and all the ancestors and their friends went flying off into the wind and back to nature. Tera devoted her life to taking care of her beloved dogs, but this was the day for them to take care of her.

You now have knowledge that grieving is a normal human process in what for you may be an abnormal situation. You see how grief can differ from one person to the next, one situation to the next. You grudgingly accept that life as you have known it is irretrievably changed forever. Are you ready now to learn how the type of loss you have experienced impacts the progression of your new normal?

Chapter 3

Impact from Types of Loss

Have you experienced an anticipated loss or a sudden loss? Maybe you learned of a loved one's illness or injury only to lose them before you even had time to absorb the shock of the initial news. Were you blind sighted by bad news unexpectedly arriving via the internet? Do you wonder how each of these experiences affects people who are grieving—people like you?

In this chapter you will learn about reactions to different types of losses. You will gain knowledge of what makes anticipated versus sudden losses different from one another, and what you can expect to experience from each. The newest way of learning of a loss by reading it online will be explored. You will read about reactions and suggestions that have worked for other grieving people to hopefully help ease you through your own pain.

The First of Two Evils—Anticipated Loss

While losing a loved one under any circumstance is never easy, it is a very different experience to witness the dying process from a terminal illness than if that same person were to die suddenly. Knowing someone you love is dying gives you choices, as difficult as they may be. You can choose if and when to be present with the patient, choose if you will call in clergy and who you want that person to be, act on behalf of your loved one by following expressed and written instructions through Advance Directives, Do Not Resuscitate orders (DNR), and/or a Living Will, and more.

An anticipated death allows friends and family to come together in a supportive and loving community. It gives you and your loved ones a chance to say good-bye in what can be a very healing and even beautiful experience. Some have described being present at a loved one's passing as a more spiritual experience than giving birth to a child.

Having time to say the things you want and need to say, or simply to listen when a dying loved one speaks can be deeply meaningful. Every minute, every word, and every action can be profound as memories are created to ease you through the difficult days that lay ahead.

Amy's Story—A Few Words Can Mean So Much

Amy lay in Intensive Care, unable to speak, after what would ultimately prove to be a fatal stroke. Struggling to get a message through to her family, she finally wrote a note in barely legible handwriting. Her last written request she worked so hard to deliver? "Please let work know I won't be there." An impeccable work ethic to her final days, Amy was easily reassured by her loving children that the call had already been made. And then she rested. As is so often the case, small things really do mean so much.

My Comments on Amy's Story

Often well-intentioned loved ones will reassure the patient that everything will be all right and that they are going to be fine. Maybe it's because they believe it's true, maybe it's because they want it to be true, or maybe it's because it makes them feel better to say it. Regardless of the reason, the problem with minimizing the seriousness of a potentially life ending situation is that the patient's wishes may not be heard, or may even be dismissed. Had Amy's children not been willing to listen rather than reassure, they may never have known what was so important to their mother or been able to act on her behalf in a way that meant so much to her.

Bumps in the Road

Of course, not all expected deaths or the situations surrounding them go smoothly. If the dying person was difficult to deal with when healthy, they can be more than difficult when they aren't. Keeping the focus on the person being honored at the end of a lifetime can provide direction and perspective during times that may challenge you the most.

Mary's Story—No Good Deed Goes Unpunished

Mary was a kind and generous woman. After her mother's death, she took over the role of caregiver for her more than cantankerous old grandmother. Nana was famous for being a master manipulator, often using guilt and a sharp tongue as her favorite weapons. It was clear she had received better than she had given, first from her daughter and then from her daughter's daughter.

Nana's always difficult personality became even more exasperating when the time came that Mary was no longer able to care for her at home. Despite many years of selfless devotion to her grandmother, Mary blamed herself for her grandmother's failing health.

My Comments to Mary—Trading Guilt for Peace of Mind

I asked Mary what had happened that prevented her from bringing her grandmother back home to live. She explained how Nana had collapsed in her bedroom, her bodily functions failed, and even the paramedics who came to the house struggled to move her from the home to the ambulance. Efforts to stabilize her in a care facility resulted in re-hospitalization each time, ultimately being placed into hospice care.

Even at this point, Mary struggled with guilt, feeling she should do more. I asked what other options there were to care for her grandmother and she was clear—there were none. She shared many

ll things her grandmother said that wounded Mary so
said she realized her Nana's words were deliberately
en by her own years of unhappiness. After thoughtful
tion, Mary accepted that she had done all she could do
and the only thing that gave Nana's hurtful words power was Mary's
own reaction.

Mary traded guilt for peace of mind and declared she would no
longer let Nana's words wound her. She found comfort in the knowledge she had done her best and her mother would have been proud
of her for giving so much to someone she knew was so difficult.

The Conclusion of Mary's Story

Mary continued to visit her grandmother every day, dodging continued insults and accusations. As she was leaving one evening, Mary
said, "Good-night, Nana. I love you. See you tomorrow." And with
that, the old woman let loose.

"It's your fault I'm here! You could take me home if you wanted!
See me tomorrow? I might be dead by then!" Mary calmly looked
at her grandmother and said, "Then I won't see you. I love you,
Nana. Good night."

Proactive Grief Is a Thief

Proactive grief means you withdraw from the patient, from your
loved one, by distancing yourself both physically and emotionally
in an effort to avoid the pain when a loss is imminent. You may
visit less often, keep yourself busy with distractions, or find excuses
why you aren't available. When you are there, you may feel anxious
and find yourself chattering about mindless subjects or staying busy
with meaningless tasks.

While your reactions may be normal, the problem with proactive grief is it is a thief. It robs both you and your loved one of the
precious little time you do have left. Consciously or not, choosing
to avoid pain only means you are choosing not to acknowledge it,
not that it isn't there.

Staying present and focused demands your strength and your courage, but the rewards can be great. You are completely present with and for the person you love while they are still with you. There will be plenty of time for grieving all too soon.

The "D" Word

The "D" word—death, dying, died, dead—is the proverbial elephant in the living room. When someone is dying, often people are afraid or just don't want or know how to talk about death. It's as if using the word has the power to provoke the very thing you want to avoid.

If you find yourself in this situation and don't know what to do or say, there's good news. You don't have to say anything, just listen. If the person who is ill needs and wants to talk about death, providing witness can be a special gift from you to your loved one. You may even be amazed at what you hear.

What Do I Do when Someone I Love Is Dying?

- *Allow yourself to participate in your grief community,* those around you who share your loss. Tell stories, share fond memories, cry and laugh together.
- *Take turns sitting with the patient.* Allow each caregiver time together with the patient and rest time alone.
- *Do not try to fix the problem.* This is not a puzzle to be solved; it is an experience to be lived.
- *Know that just because a death is expected, it doesn't mean you shouldn't feel sad.* Even when a death seems to be a relief for a suffering loved one, it is still normal to be sad and feel the vast emptiness that is left behind.
- *Recognize how your life changes instantly if you were the primary caregiver.* Your 24/7 role changes to zero in a moment, demanding a major life adjustment on top of your grief. Expect to be beyond physically exhausted after a long period of poor quality and frequently interrupted sleep and performing the intense demands of care giving.

- *Do not blame yourself if your loved one passes the one minute you have left the room.* There are many theories about why this happens, but the fact is, it happens. Focus on the times you were there and not the one minute you were not.

The Other Evil—Sudden Loss

Sudden loss is a trauma. It is an assault to all your senses affecting your emotional, physical and spiritual well being. From one moment to the next, sudden loss changes your world forever. There is no choice. There is no compromise.

Your brain is slammed into shock. Food in your stomach instantly sours. You may fall to your knees, completely unable to support your own weight. The desperate need to do something is trumped only by the fact you are powerless to do anything at all.

There is simply no way to prepare for this type of loss. Etched into eternal memory is that one phone call, that ominous knock on the door, that impersonal but too-familiar image on the 6 o'clock news. Your mind is screaming, "This isn't happening!" when clearly your body knows that it is.

Reactive Grief

Reactive grief is ruthless. It is demanding, inflexible, and relentless. It discriminates against no one. There is nothing that can be said or done to change what has happened. Actions don't matter. Words of comfort mean nothing. Whatever you need to do to survive is exactly what you need to do.

What Do I Do After a Sudden Loss?

- *Understand that in the beginning if you are breathing and walking at the same time you are doing great.*
- *Make the necessary phone calls sharing the bad news,* if possible. This can help begin to bring some reality to your situation, allow you to feel somewhat productive, and pull

your support community together quickly. If you don't want to or can't make the calls, assign the job to the person you want to do this for you.

- *Call the experts.* You may be required to make some big decisions in a short period of time, and possibly in areas where you have little or no expertise. Estate attorneys, financial advisors, hospice staff, counselors, funeral directors can all provide critical information and skilled help. Choose people you feel confident will act in your best interest and let them do what they are there to do.
- *Do not be fooled by superficial kindness from the media.* If they are there, it is for no reason other than the story. Try to be as boring as possible.

Death by Internet

With the advent of the World Wide Web has come a world wide array of new ways we can receive bad news. From global events to losses that hit us on a very personal level, digitally receiving catastrophic news is challenging many of us in a way we have never experienced before.

Our bodies and our minds are not designed to absorb, let alone process information received in this inhuman way. It is even possible to learn of a death that causes a sudden loss reaction long after the death actually occurred. Where is the framework to even begin to know how to deal with a loss discovered in this cold-blooded way?

Turning to online "friends" for support can just make matters worse. Clever cartoon faces, superficial words or poems, or a well-intentioned cyber hug will never replace being wrapped up in warm, supportive and loving arms.

You Have Mail—Rose's Story

There was nothing special going on for Rose at work this one particular day. She was on her lunch break with time to kill when she decided to check her email. She was surprised to see a very business-like message waiting for her from the company her good friend and former colleague owned. They had one of those decades-long friend-ships where they didn't speak often but when they did it was as if no time had passed, so this formal and impersonal message was odd.

Rose thought maybe her friend had decided to retire and sold his company without telling her. So, she did what people do in this day and age of technology—she searched on the internet looking for news. Nothing prepared her for what instantly appeared right in front of her eyes.

There it was, big as you please, an article on a giant fundraising event in honor of her friend. Not only had he died, but several months had passed since his death and she knew nothing about it until this very moment. Rose stared at the computer in utter dis-belief, unable to even catch her breath.

Rose's lunch break was over and it was time to go back to work. She had a meeting scheduled with a client, no time to cancel and no time for emotions. She needed to function as if nothing had happened when, in fact, a lot had happened. She didn't know what to do but with her mind spinning, she conducted her meeting as if that was the only important thing on the agenda that day.

Rose later learned her friend had been sick for a while. No one told her he was ill because they all assumed she knew—after all, it was posted on social media. There was no picking up the phone, no getting on a plane to go help, no attending a funeral or memorial service with friends who shared the loss. Even the big event Rose read about that sad day was months in the past.

Not only did Rose feel deep pain at news of the death of her friend, she felt forgotten by all her other colleagues and friends who never thought it strange when they didn't hear from her. Rose says her loss still does not seem real to her. She feels like she can just pick up the phone and talk with her dear friend, but she never makes that call because her loss is just real enough to know he will never answer again.

"What If" Game

Sudden losses set survivors up for asking themselves endless rounds of "What If" and "If Only" questions. Asking these questions and playing out scenarios that might have yielded a different outcome is only natural, but these are questions with no good answers.

- I went to visit my aunt and was surprised at how much weight she'd gained. I didn't want to say anything because that would be rude. I learned too late that she hadn't gained weight; she was retaining fluids because she was in congestive heart failure. If only I had said something...
- We knew my adult daughter had a serious illness and was going through an especially tough couple days. I kept the grandkids quiet and away from the bedroom, never knowing what we would find when we went in to check on her. What if I had just gone in sooner...?
- Mom was getting up in years so I wasn't completely shocked to get the news that she had fallen. I offered to get on a plane immediately, but she insisted she was fine and had only a bit of a headache. Mom never wanted me to worry and I was surprised when I later learned she hit her head when she fell. If I had only gone there and taken her to the doctor myself...

You can ask yourself an infinite number of these questions, but the only logical and factual response is that you did not know. You can never know what might have happened if you had had different information, knowledge or made a different choice.

Have you ever noticed how "What If" questions only get asked when something bad happens while good outcomes get taken for granted? You would never comment to your family, "I'm sure glad we left the restaurant when we did so we could make it home without getting into an accident!" Wouldn't that be silly?

⁊

With your growing knowledge about how grief works, how your old normal is in the past, and how different types of loss can impact reactions, it's time to look at how the specific relationship to the person who died may be influencing you in your grief process.

Chapter 4

Loss by Type of Relationship

Was your loss a parent? A sibling? A friend? Have you considered how your specific relationship to the person who died might be affecting your grief? Maybe you are struggling to put your present feelings into perspective compared to other deaths you may have experienced in the past. You might be trying to support someone you love who is grieving, searching for the right words to say or the helpful thing to do.

This chapter examines some of the more common losses many if not most of us will face at some point in our lives. Entire books have been written on each one of these types of losses, but here we briefly consider what makes one different from another and how they may be affecting you or others near you.

Parent Loss

The knowledge we will most likely outlive our parents does not ensure we are remotely prepared for the eventual reality. Age of the child at the time of the parent's death yields very different effects and challenges. The quality of the relationship to the deceased parent also plays a key role in how loss is experienced and processed.

Young Child Loss of a Parent—Explaining death to a child is never easy, even if it's the family gold fish on its way to eternity via a bathroom flush. Truthful but age appropriate answers work best. If you aren't sure, let the child ask questions to guide you through the answers they need and are ready to hear. Then, ask the child to explain back to you what they heard to make sure the communication had the desired result.

A three-year old demanded an immediate answer to his question. "Where is he?" Rather than try to explain death to a small child, his grandmother asked, "Where do YOU think he is?" The frowning boy thought for a moment and then broke into a big smile. "I think he's in the moon and the stars!" That seemed as good an answer as any.

Talking to children about death can demand some creative communication. However, care should be exercised in limiting the use of magical answers and stories designed to appease young children's concerns and questions. Complicated adult logic and the pure, simple logic of a child are not remotely the same.

Alice's Story—The Dangers of Magical Thinking

Six-year-old Alice's grandfather had just died after a lengthy battle with cancer. Caring friends and neighbors worked to reassure Alice by saying that Grandpa was an angel now. They told her he would always be with her and would look out for her for the rest of her life. All she had to do was talk to him and he would hear every word. Visibly troubled, Alice was not remotely comforted by these words. In fact, the resulting effect was quite the opposite.

A few days after the death, a family member found a letter the grandfather had written as he was dying. It was his confession to his family that he had sexually molested his granddaughter, Alice, and several other young girls. The family members were understandably distraught and immediately sought counseling together and individually for Alice.

Alice came into the therapy room agitated and anxious. She did not make eye contact and stayed distracted by fidgeting with toys in the room. Finally settling down, she looked up with unforgettable and frightened big blue eyes. Summoning up great strength and courage for such a little girl, Alice gave voice to her dread. "Now that he's an angel, he can find me and hurt me whenever he wants."

Instead of the idea of a grandpa as an ever-present being offering comfort to a small child, the very idea brought sheer terror. Who would literally think an angel could follow you and hurt you whenever it wanted? A six year old who trusted the adults around her to take care of her and tell her the truth.

Susan's Story—More Magical Thinking

Susan was only 5 when her mother was killed in a car accident. She repeatedly asked adults around her where her mother was and all gave the same and only answer they knew. "She's in heaven now."

Susan was later caught climbing trees to dangerous heights, sometimes using ladders. The behaviors continued over time and when she was old enough to be able to climb out of her bedroom window and onto the roof, the adults sought counseling and Susan was declared to be a high suicide risk.

Many years later Susan was in therapy dealing with unresolved issues she had relating to the loss of her mother at such a young age. The adult Susan explained with complete clarity, she was never suicidal. She believed what the adults said about Mom being in heaven and she was determined to climb up there to be with her. Climbing trees and scaling roofs seemed the logical way to do it.

> *Older Child Loss of a Parent*—Adults will often isolate children from death-related events in an effort to protect them. These are irreversible decisions made with surely the best of intentions, but the results may yield less than desirable results.

Nikki's Story—Lost in Time

Nikki was a 30-something woman coming to therapy after a series of failed relationships, all with endings she had initiated. When asked for some details on her family history, Nikki shared she was a young pre-teen when she lost her father to a heart attack. She began to sob, rocked back and forth, held herself tightly and worked hard just to breathe.

Nikki described having been called to the principal's office where her uncle was waiting to take her home. She knew she must have done something horribly wrong for her uncle's unprecedented appearance. His ominous silence on the drive home just proved she had to be in really big trouble. Nikki was more confused when they arrived at her house and her parents were not there. Her uncle flatly told Nikki that her father had died, that Mommy was resting, and that she needed to be a good girl and go to her room and do her homework.

When Nikki's father died, she was developmentally at an age where dads walk on water and can do no wrong. From that point forward, no man Nikki ever met came close to measuring up to the ultimate gold standard, namely her dad. Nikki was an adult still struggling to understand what she had done wrong that memorable day, believing events beyond her control were her fault. Inside her adult body was a very sad young girl.

Efforts to protect Nikki from catastrophic events in this case clearly did more harm than good. No one will ever know exactly how the outcome would have been different had other choices been made, but including and reassuring Nikki as part of the grieving family rather than isolating her may have at least kept her from feeling so guilty and so very alone.

Teen Loss of a Parent—Losing a parent as a teen can propel a young person into adulthood quickly and way ahead of schedule. Treating the teen like a child at this critical time will likely result in resentment and rebellion, making a bad situation even worse.

On the flip side, telling an adolescent boy who has just lost his father he is now "the man of the family" places a burden on the boy that is far beyond his reach and his role, and at the worst possible time. How could a boy even know what that means? This seems to be an assignment given only to male children. Have you ever heard a girl being told she is now "the woman of the family?"

Has the teen been allowed to make choices and participate in events surrounding the death? Has the teen been asked in what ways he or she would like to participate, or not participate? Involvement in the planning, rituals and the support network can be healthy and empowering for a young person introduced to grief with a first loss that is so profoundly significant.

Adult Loss of a Parent—The affect of parent loss on us as adult children is complicated, at best. It comes with layers of meaning and emotional effects based on the quality of the relationship over the course of a lifetime.

You may experience little emotion with the death of a parent with whom you were not close. On the other hand, you can be beyond devastated after the death of a cherished parent; a loss that can take years to assimilate because the absence is so great. You could even be surprised to find yourself processing strong feelings, ranging from love to hate, for a parent with whom you had a conflicted relationship.

One reaction that does seem to be universal when looking at the world for the first time with no living parent somewhere on the planet is the introduction to your own mortality. People of all ages describe themselves as "orphans," now the oldest living generation.

Spouse or Partner Loss

Regardless of how a spouse died, suddenly or after a long illness, surely there is no more indisputable dose of reality than waking up alone in a bed you have shared every night with the person you vowed to love, honor and cherish. "Until death do us part" are no longer just words people say, rather they are a powerful descriptor that says when and how marriages end, by necessity and not choice.

Finding yourself a widow or widower redefines your status on every level. Married one minute and single the next? How can that be? What do you do about your wedding ring? How do you fill out forms from your doctor's office to completing your tax returns—one reminder after another as you are required to disclose your marital status? Even friendships you thought would never change often do, and through no fault or choice of your own.

For some, knowing the weight of the pain they carry means their spouse was spared facing that pain if the deaths had occurred in reverse order can bring some degree of comfort. If your marriage was rocky or had lost its sizzle, it isn't unusual to experience feelings of guilt or remorse on top of grief over things you may wish you'd done differently that are no longer possible. There are some who admit to relief an unhappy marriage is finally over, but that one doesn't seem to be talked about in public very often. Just as each relationship is unique to the particular couple, so is each loss.

While the death of a partner in a committed but unmarried relationship can be just as profoundly devastating and life altering, acknowledgement and support of the loss can be a very different experience from that of married counterparts. Forms still get filled out the same way as before, jewelry remains unchanged and unchallenged, and tax status is unaffected. Even bereavement groups for grieving spouses may not fit comfortably for the grieving partner. This could explain why some grief counselors in private practice settings report seeing more bereaved partners than spouses in treatment, but there is no way to know for certain as no reliable statistics even exist on partner loss.

Harry's Story—Invalid and Invisible

Harry and Linda had been happily together for many years. They had a healthy relationship, a loving family, a beautiful home, and owned a successful business together. Both having experienced past divorces, neither felt particularly motivated to get married or even make it a priority. Legal chores got put off indefinitely, including creating wills.

Linda was out enjoying her favorite hobby one day, flying her small plane, when a freak accident caused the plane to crash suddenly ending her life. When the authorities called the family with the news and immediate tasks that had to be addressed, they did not call Harry.

Linda's relatives made all the decisions and all the arrangements for Linda's funeral and resolution of her estate. Harry was relegated to the role of observer and friend of the deceased and her legal family.

Despite the pain of losing his beloved, Harry found peace of mind in the fact that she died doing what she loved to do most. Harry was coping well with his reactions to the trauma, his many life changes, and the overwhelming financial challenges he was left to face. What Harry struggled with most was being treated as if the most significant relationship of his life was invalid and he was all but invisible.

Sibling Loss

The original love-hate relationship, for better or for worse and everything in between, we were stuck with each other from the moment the younger sibling was born. Siblings help us learn how to be in the world, how to share, how to resolve conflicts, and how to love someone we may also want to choke. On some level, we thought they'd always be there, until one day when they aren't.

Again, age at time of loss plays a key role. A 6-year old who wishes away a cute baby brother may be certain his bad wishes had something to do with his brother's death. Add only a few years to the clock and the older sibling would likely never give a thought to the possibility of his wishes having any power to actually cause a death. Add a few more years and the older sibling would know that if all of us who have younger siblings could have wished them away when we were little, there probably wouldn't be many little brothers or sisters left.

Until more recently, books and research on sibling loss were all but non-existent. It was almost as if surviving a sibling was an insignificant life event, the furthest thing from the truth. New research and expanding publications are offering increasing recognition and consideration of this major type of loss.

Friend Loss

Who do you turn to when you lose a good friend? This was the person who you told your deepest darkest secrets, someone who really knew you, shared your laughter and your tears. This was the person you could always count on to be there for you. This is the person you chose to be family.

Ideally, the relatives of your friend acknowledge and honor the important role you played in their loved one's life. Hopefully you are welcome as a member of the bereaved family. Unfortunately, this is not always the case. The family may not even know you or recognize you in the crowd.

In reality, you may be the best person in the entire world to know your friend's wishes and beliefs. You may be a connection for your friend's child or children to share stories and memories of their loved one like no one else can.

Find where you fit in, where you are welcome and needed, and where you want and need to be. If necessary, consider a separate celebration or private memorial with other friends who share your loss. If you are alone in this loss, consider having your own private ritual just for you.

Pet Loss—A Silence So Loud

Did you ever think a house could be so quiet? Where are the jangling tags or the click-click of nails hitting the floor? What would you give to be able to shush a bark or trip over a silly toy? How about another sloppy kiss received with feigned disgust?

For those of us who love our animals, when we lose them it can be like losing a member of our family. The grief is just as real and can be just as deep as it is for any human loss, for some even greater.

Never before have we lived our lives in such isolation, many even living the dream of working from home. Visiting a friend or relative now often means getting on an airplane instead of just jumping in the car to meet for lunch. We sit in front of our computers and our phones doing "social networking," and more of us are living single than ever before. Is it any wonder our pets have become so important? This is love that is constant, undemanding, and unconditional.

What Do I Do?

- *Find fellow pet lovers to support you.*
- *Avoid anyone who attempts to question, criticize or fix your pain,* especially if they think they need to buy you a new pet to cheer you up.
- *Make no apologies for your sadness* that is just as valid as another person's sadness.
- *If someone asks you what's wrong and you don't want to go into details, usually a simple "someone in my family died" will suffice,* and it is the truth.
- *Consider having your own ritual to say good-bye,* maybe releasing balloons or scattering ashes somewhere special.
- Put a favorite picture that makes you smile where it is often and easily seen.
- *Stay out of pet shops* where there are radars that identify grieving pet owners with credit cards as prime targets for the next big sale—and there is always a big sale.
- *When the time comes to bring a new pet into your home, consider choosing a different gender, color, or even breed* so your new companion gets a fresh start and you avoid having a reminder of the pet you are missing.

✢

You now have a perspective on your grief process. You've considered the degree of change that has occurred in your life, and you have a greater understanding of how the relationship to the person who has died may affect your emotions. Next we look at complications that can occur with grief and loss that may not be anticipated or recognized, but can greatly impact your experience.

Chapter 5

Detours on the Way to a New Normal

Have you found yourself blind sighted by how far the effects of your loss can reach? Maybe you thought you were through the most difficult days only to be surprised when more of them showed up, where and when least expected.

Now it's time to look at the lingering after effects of loss. These are the recurring, often unexpected challenges of coping with loss that can continue after the funeral is over and the visitors have long gone home. This is the stuff most people around you never think of, and you are seldom allowed to forget.

I Quit

Grieving is hard work. It is a full time job and your resignation will not be accepted. Imagine a job where you are required to work every day around the clock without a single day off. You may get an occasional break, but then it's right back to work. Picture yourself waving good-bye to your co-workers as they head off for a fun weekend while you sit there all alone, doing your best to just keep going. It isn't fair, it doesn't feel good, and it is beyond exhausting. That job is called Grief.

It's Raining Losses

A graduate student asked for an interview for a paper she was writing on grief and loss. She asked good and thoughtful questions and with five minutes remaining she said she had one more question. "Is there any such thing as secondary loss?" With that question on the table, the interview did not end on schedule.

Secondary losses are all the new and additional losses that result from the primary loss. The list of secondary losses can be a long one and is largely why we don't just "get over it." There is never just one "it."

Parents who lose a young child, for example, do not suffer only that loss. Gone is the naïve belief that parents do not outlive their children. Lost is the experience of watching that child grow up, graduate high school, go to college and become an adult. Non-negotiable is the fact there will be no grandchildren from that child. Where is the smiling face of that handsome son or beautiful daughter when you celebrate your Golden Wedding Anniversary?

The pain of secondary losses can occur even if you were not present or actively involved with the original loss. An infant's parent could die without having any directly conscious effect on the child. Yet, as that child grows, the impact of the parent's absence grows, too. It's there in Kindergarten when other kids ask where your mom or dad is. It's there when you look in the mirror and wonder if you look like your parent, or perhaps know that you do from pictures. It's there when you star in the school play, when you graduate from college, on your wedding day, and the day you welcome your baby into the world. The list is endless because the losses are endless.

Secondary Losses are Sneaky!

Just about the time you start to feel your new normal settling in, the future comes sneaking up on you. The full realization that this life change is permanent begins to sink in. Whether you like it or not, life starts to change as new things happen and new events occur.

Fay was buying a car after her old one had been damaged in an accident. She was pleased with the great deal she was able to negotiate for a fabulous new car on the last day of the year. She went to remove her belongings from the old car, preparing for the exchange, when out of the blue Fay was caught completely off guard with an overwhelming rush of emotions. Suddenly, it hit her. She was surrendering the car that drove her dear one to the hospital one very dark night, a car ride that proved to be the last he would ever have. Unable to contain her heartache, embarrassing or not, right in the middle of a car dealership she began to sob.

Now, you might think it's silly, even ridiculous to cry over a car, especially when you're getting a really cool brand new one. But, it was never about the car—it was about what the car represented. Trading the old car for the new was indisputable proof that life and time go on. It was about losing one more piece, one more connection to someone already too far away. It was about more sadness when it was expected least.

New Normal Tips

Expect the unexpected. Know that secondary losses will continue to occur indefinitely. Some of your responses may be expected but many will be a surprise. There is nothing wrong with you, even though at times you may feel like there is. The more you resist or ignore your feelings, the tougher the work tends to be. The more you go with the emotions, let yourself feel what you feel, the sooner you will be back on your path, moving forward to your new normal.

What Do Dirty Laundry and Unresolved Grief Have In Common?

They both pile up! And at some point in time, they both can be pretty difficult to ignore.

When you experience a new loss, it's inevitable that you will compare the new loss to losses you have experienced in the past. The reactions and emotions become increasingly familiar despite the fact each loss is unique. You may find yourself surprised how a new loss can tap into any unresolved issues you may have from a prior loss, issues you may not have realized remained.

Even if you have managed to hold your grief at bay, the accumulation still occurs. Significant losses that have not been grieved may be tucked away on some shelf, but eventually the shelf tends to get too full and can come crashing down. Even a small loss that may seem relatively insignificant can be enough to trigger an avalanche of stored-up emotions.

Steve's Story—The Cowboy and the Baby Chick

Steve was a strapping middle-aged cowboy, tough on the outside and tender in the middle. He was in therapy dealing with some relationship issues, but one day he arrived with a very different problem. He was distraught. This big, strong guy was in tears as he shared the news that his dog had just killed a baby chick.

It was touching to see how much this man cared about animals, but at some point the grief seemed to be disproportionate to the event. Steve had grown up on a farm with lots of animals and surely this could not have been the first time he'd witnessed a farm animal tragedy. It seemed like there might be something else going on.

Steve was asked if anything else had happened that day or if it was a birthday or anniversary of any significant day or event. He seemed perplexed at the question and thought about it for a long time. Finally he said that it was the anniversary of his brother's death, a death he had never faced let alone grieved. When asked if he thought it was possible that his brother's death might have something to do with the painful emotions he was facing that day, without hesitation and shaking his head, Steve said, "Nope."

Closure Confusion

What does "closure" mean? What does it look like and how do you get it? How do you know that you have it? Can it open back up once it's closed?

The concept of closure is another example of a useful concept that has been generically applied to so many situations that it has become difficult if not impossible to effectively define. Everyone wants it, others urge you to get it, and you may seek it without really knowing what it is.

Some professionals working in the area of grief and loss have chosen to stop using the word "closure" all together because it has become so confusing. While it seems the actual word choice leaves something to be desired, the fact remains that the concept is valid and plays an important role in accepting a loss and addressing the intense emotions of grief.

Closure can be a feeling. Closure can be a fact. Closure can be an event. You may even have had closure, then some new information surfaces that creates new questions or issues you are unable to directly address, effectively creating a new need for closure.

Just as "letting go" means letting go of your old normal and not of your loved one, "closure" means you are only closing loose ends that may be associated with your loss. Resolving loose ends allows you to remove complications and distractions related to your loss so you can move forward in a less restricted, less burdened, and healthier way.

Closure means different things to different people in different situations. What is right for you may not be right for someone else. What works today may not work later, or vice versa. Not only the definition is unique to each individual and each situation, but so is the method of achievement.

Chris' Story—Closure Is In the Eye of the Beholder

Chris had an embittered relationship with her father. It seemed holding onto his anger had always been more valuable to the father than having a relationship with any of his children. Chris had repeatedly done her best, but the results had been consistently poor.

The day came when the father's death was imminent and Chris felt obligated to participate in the family's death watch. The man had delivered a lifetime of relentless emotional and physical cruelties to his entire family, and in his final hours he asked for forgiveness. Without hesitation, Chris responded, "Too little, too late."

Some may be quick to judge Chris harshly in this situation while others may applaud her for having the courage of her convictions. Until a person has walked in your shoes, who is to say? For Chris, she was being true to herself by refusing to grant a last-minute pardon in exchange for years of abuse.

Chris was sad for the life her father lived, but she was relieved the abuse was finally over. For Chris, her father's death was her closure. For one or more of her siblings, perhaps granting the desired forgiveness was theirs.

Road Blocks to a New Normal—Lawsuits

If the loss you have experienced came with a summons, or if you are choosing to sue someone else as a result of the death of your loved one, expect major delays on your path to creating a new normal.

Not only do legal battles engulf every aspect of your life, they also keep you completely focused on the death. You will be repeating your story with lawyers, in grueling depositions, in front of a judge and maybe a jury, reciting the same story over and over. One side will work to discredit you while the other works to display your pain and suffering for all to see. You may be required to look at upsetting pictures. You may view painfully familiar articles of clothing or other personal items. You may be exposed to highly disturbing autopsy details.

If you do find yourself involved in a lawsuit, do your best to create a disaster plan, a worst-case scenario defense in case things do not go as you hope. Be sure to consider your financial needs, but focus predominantly on your own physical well-being. The best way to win is to come out with your health intact, no matter what the judge says. Once the public work is behind you, know that much of your private grief work still lies ahead.

A Giant Step to a New Normal—Funerals

Viewing a newly-dead body leaves no room for doubt about the finality of your situation. Seeing a body professionally "prepared" for a funeral may not have as strong an impact, but it is still very effective in replacing denial with a jarring dose of reality. Cremation has become very common as the choice of many, but viewing an urn of ashes can slow the acceptance of the death as your mind wrestles to connect the urn to your loved one.

The question of whether or not to view the body is frequently a point of discussion in early grief counseling. This is a decision that must be made quickly and under pressure with no options for a do over. There is no correct answer, but there is a theme in what bereaved people often report.

Many who chose or were not able to view the body later regret this choice and struggle to accept the reality that their loved one is indeed gone. This is especially true if there was a geographical separation that makes it very easy to go on as if nothing has changed. Many who were initially reluctant to view the body but changed their minds said they were glad they did. They report gaining a sense of comfort in seeing their loved one once more as a way of saying a final good-bye.

None of this is to suggest those who choose not to view the body are making a bad or wrong choice. It is simply another choice. Viewing the body of your loved one does not, however, mean that this one hard memory will or can replace a lifetime of memories. At first the death and surrounding events can seem so large it's hard to believe they could ever fade, but in time they do as happy memories begin to return once again.

Bereavement Groups

Support groups can be a wonderful resource, especially for newly bereaved people. These groups can be particularly helpful for parents who have lost children and for people who have lost loved ones through acts of violence by self or others. Finding people with whom you can speak openly about your experience and your feelings can be particularly difficult for those who have experienced a catastrophic death making a support group potentially invaluable.

If you have attended one of these groups and did not find it a helpful experience, it may simply not be the right choice of group or the right time for you. Many people come into individual therapy saying the group experience was overwhelming to them, or that they could not relate to the other people in the group or their experience. Some expressed concern that there were group members who had been attending for many years but never seemed to move past their initial loss reaction. On the other hand, there are people who come for individual counseling that report disappointing experiences with more than one therapist. They express frustration with having to start over and share their heartbreaking story with too many strangers while finding the person they feel is a match.

If you are searching for a group to attend, finding the right group for you can make the difference between a positive and a negative experience. Consider whether you prefer a peer-led group or a professionally facilitated group. If you are struggling to function in the early days of your loss, or if you are just too busy with too many things to do following your loss, finding and researching groups would be a good job for a friend who wants to be of help to you. Hospice organizations can be a good resource for learning about group options in your area. If you do not find the group process helpful, consider trying individual counseling instead. In the early days many choose to do both group and individual work, some taking a friend along for moral support until they are ready to go solo. There is no right answer. Trust that whatever option helps you is the right choice for you.

We've looked at grief and loss following the death of a loved one from multiple perspectives, but there are other losses many of us must face in our lives where there has not been a death. Next we look at divorce and then major life events from a grief and loss perspective.

Chapter 6

Significant Others

Is there anything more intoxicating than falling in love, finding that perfect partner to share your life? How exciting when the relationship continues to blossom and grow. You find yourself with your very own significant other, your spouse, your happily-ever-after person. All those feel-good chemicals are pouring into your brain. You not only don't ever want them to stop, you are so certain they never will that you swear to it in a ceremony with witnesses present to officially seal the deal. Your future has never looked brighter.

Time passes and things change, as they always do. Some relationships grow into dreams fulfilled while others go a different direction, most probably some combination of both. There are no truly reliable and consistent statistics on the success and failure rates of marriages in the US, but knowing the statistics doesn't matter much if you find yourself one of them. What happens when your significant other becomes insignificant?

Divorce Losses

It may seem odd to compare the death of a loved one to the death of a marriage, but the two have a lot in common. A divorce is a death, the death of the marriage. It is the end of a dream once held sacred. Whether it is the signature of a coroner on a death certificate or the judge on a divorce decree declaring you are no longer married, life will never be the same again.

Loss of Best Friend—Regardless of how you now feel about your ex, there was a time when he or she was your best friend. This was the person you woke up with in the morning, told the details of your day, shared your popcorn with at the movies, and fell asleep with at night. A marriage where spouses fail to become genuine friends is a marriage at risk, but a divorce from the person who was once your best friend is a heartache you fear will never end.

Loss of Trust—One could probably make at least a decent argument against blindly trusting another person. Great idea or not, losing trust, losing innocence, is emotionally expensive. Not only can it cause you to look at others with mistrust, it can make you question even your own judgement. People often say, "Trust your heart," but isn't that what got you to where you are now?

Loss of Hope—For many divorcing people, hope for some intervention or new awareness, just a chance—any chance, continues up to the very last moment before the divorce is final. Holding the actual signed papers in your hand is rarely a time for celebration. Yet it is grieving the loss of this hope that opens the door to new hopes and new possibilities for a healthier and happier future.

Loss of Privacy—You may be asking how you somehow became the star of your own reality TV show. There you and your ex are on social media, including pictures you didn't want to see and opinions you didn't solicit. You can't ignore the looks when you show up at an event or the way conversation stops when you arrive. From the news via the internet to a PTA meeting, just when you want to fade into the woodwork you have become the center of attention.

Loss of an Intact Family—A divorce by deliberate design means a family is now divided and all members will be challenged to find their new place in this redesigned version of the family that used to be. This is a daunting process if both spouses mutually agreed to divorce, but it can be brutal if one spouse wanted out and the other did not.

Divorced families with young children will now evolve into two separate households, each led by two independent decision makers, often with two sets of rules, and clothes that travel with kids or maybe even a different wardrobe at each house. Holidays and birthdays need to be reconfigured and can quickly change again as children age and the divorced family finds its new equilibrium.

While the kids are busy trying to figure out how to adapt to their new circumstances, parents are doing the same thing. You may have been a parent that stayed on top of the household 24/7 but now you find yourself alone in a quiet house half the time, not quite sure what to do or how to act. Or, you may be a parent who wasn't heavily involved in the family or the children's schedules but now find yourself with a new job as a parent on top of the one you already had. Whatever the particular circumstances and whether you knew what you were signing up for or not, a new normal is forming right in front of your eyes.

Divorced families with adult children have plenty of adjusting to do as well. Which house do they go to and when? What is okay to say and what isn't? If one child physically favors one parent, is that now an issue for the other parent? What pictures do you hang on the wall or leave hanging on the wall, and which do you take down? If grandchildren are part of the family, or soon to be, what is a healthy and loving way to raise them with respect for divorced grandparents?

In-laws also get reshuffled in a divorce, extended family now burdened with trying to figure out their new role in this changed family system. You may be sad to lose the relationship you once had with your in-laws or it may be a relief to see them go with the ex, but either way these relationships are also changing and will take some figuring out for everyone.

At some point, one or both exes will meet new people, start new relationships, maybe remarry and even have more children. Blended families can challenge the best of divorces with the addition of new members into the existing divorced family system. The word "blended" is an excellent descriptor because both the original family members and the new family members, from partners to kids to extended family, will be in the position of needing to compromise on culture, tradition, boundaries and mysteries yet to be revealed.

Reversing Significant

Once someone has transitioned from stranger to friend to significant other to spouse, it can be difficult if not impossible to reverse the person back to insignificant other. The connection changes but at least some remnants remain, especially when children are involved.

While going back to neutral once that connection has been made may not be an available option, putting the relationship into perspective in the big picture of life is a good and healthy option you can choose. It may seem hard to believe in the beginning, but hopefully the day will not be far off until your new life is going so well you never give a thought to what even qualifies another person as significant or not.

What Do I Do?

- While the death of a spouse is not the same thing as a divorce, a divorce is nonetheless a major loss for most people. *Give yourself time and permission to grieve the heartache you are facing.* Remember, there is no "getting over it" because there isn't ever one "it."

- *Look back for lessons learned and forward to better days ahead* with greater wisdom and maturity at your disposal. A mistake is not defined by getting a divorce or ending a relationship, rather it is by repeating destructive old patterns as a result of life lessons not learned or ignored.
- *If there are children involved, helping them to feel loved and safe is one thing both parents likely agree on with unified conviction.* When you and your ex like each other the least, it is a good time to look at the children you created together and love them the most. Consider including a Co-Parenting Agreement as part of your divorce mediation to prevent problems before they arise. (A guide is provided in Reinventing Normal: How Choice and Change Shape Our Lives by this author.)
- *Surround yourself with supportive and caring friends.* These are the people who will listen while you cry or rant or will hand you the spoon if you need to eat an entire container of ice cream, but they are also the ones who will talk you into taking a shower and getting out of the house. People who relish in your angst and love to gossip about your divorce drama are voyeurs, not to be confused with real friends.
- *Consider taking several months or even a year off from romance.* First get to know yourself post-divorce before trying to know someone else. Think of some of the nice things you used to do for your now ex and now do them for you. Buy yourself flowers, a nice piece of jewelry, prepare your favorite meal or shop for a new outfit. Have you ever taken and really enjoyed a vacation alone? Maybe it's time to try it. Learn to be your own best friend.
- *When the time does comes that you meet someone new you think you may like, slow is the way to go.* Take time getting to know

one another. Limit the number and length of dates in the beginning as well as texting and phone calls. Find out who this person is first—values, beliefs, availability, communication—and then figure out if he or she might be a good match for you. The foundation of a great marriage is a solid friendship, an investment well worth making.

Breaking up really is hard to do, a broken heart more than an expression or song. As difficult as it may be and as long as it may take, this is a story where you get to write the ending. Single or married, children or no children, young or old, your next story just might be your happily ever after.

Chapter 7

Other Losses

Have you ever considered how much of your life has been affected by loss? Have you considered how many things you gave up to make space for something or someone new? Maybe you are surprised to find yourself experiencing feelings you recognize as grief, yet no one close to you has died.

Two therapists known for their work in grief and loss were giving a joint presentation to a large audience of fellow mental health professionals. Questions were addressed in the final segment and both presenters were visibly surprised with a question from one of the participants. "How have you two been able to focus your work for so long and with so many people in this difficult subject area?" Both presenters looked at one another, then turned back to the audience and in unison said, "It's all grief and loss work."

Loss of Financial Well-Being

Loss of Job—It doesn't matter if you lost your job through no fault of your own, the impact can still be devastating. You are faced with the need to find another job when you may have been perfectly happy with the one you had. You may suffer financial hardship with time off between jobs, or you may find yourself forced to accept a position for less money than you were making before. In a tough economy, it can be a struggle to find any job when having no job is simply not an option.

If you lost your job because you were fired, there is typically an additional layer of trauma to address. You may be angry, embarrassed, ashamed, frightened, depressed, to name some of the typical emotions. Finding new work is likely even more challenging in this situation.

New Normal Tips

Fake it until you make it. It's easy to get discouraged after you lose a job for any reason, but giving up is not a solution. The best way not to get hired when you do make it to an interview is to present yourself as depressed, hopeless, desperate, or angry. Focus your time and energy on being ready to snag that perfect—or at least good enough—job when it comes your way.

Loss of Career—A career is something you choose carefully, study and learn about to gain expertise, and work hard to grow and develop. It is a reflection of your personality and how you likely identify yourself in public. A career can be a dream realized. Is it any wonder that losing a career through industry obsolescence, forced retirement, illness or any other involuntary means is such a life-altering event?

New Normal Tips

Keep looking forward for momentum and back only for foundation. Get curious and stay interested. Keep learning to keep your mind active and your expertise growing, no matter what your age. Focus on what you do well, where you have succeeded, then lead with your strengths and your head held high.

Loss of Business—If you owned your own business and that business was closed because of financial failure, or taken over for any reason against your will, the loss can be crippling on every possible level.

Your business is not who you are as a person, but it is an entity you nurtured into reality from only a vision—your vision. It is a relationship. What you grew and likely hoped to sell some day for a sizeable profit to create a cozy retirement nest egg, or pass off to your next generation, may have disappeared in a puff of smoke.

It may not be fair, and it sure isn't easy, but it's time to write another business plan. You did it before, so you know how to do it again, only better. You may want to change careers, retire, open a different new business, relocate, hire an expert to help you, go back to school to learn new or enhance existing skills. The sky is the limit and the goal is to choose your direction deliberately and purposefully. Get excited about your future again!

New Normal Tips

Just as buying or starting a business is never a surprise, neither is a business closing. Your best line of defense is to start early to create your "What Next Plan." If your initial plan is nothing more than ideas and busy tasks scribbled on a napkin, beginning to envision a new future can make the difference between positive forward thinking and sinking into a depression just when you need your motivation most.

When major corporations make large reductions in workforces, most avoid making announcements on a Friday. Sending newly unemployed workers out the door with such disturbing news to face a weekend does not bode well. What corporations do instead is announce layoffs or closings first thing on a Monday morning and immediately send the newly unemployed workers to a busy schedule of benefits counseling, resume writing, and workshops teaching interviewing skills. Staying busy and being productive becomes the new full-time job until replaced by a new paying job.

New Normal Tips

Always keep your job search records. Whenever you do a job search you make invaluable networking contacts. You find out what works for you, and you gain job seeking skills and practice. You likely wrote a dozen versions of your resume, each just as difficult to complete as the last—keep them all. Making a record and copies of all your activities can pay off should you find yourself back in the search process again, voluntarily or not.

Work Now, Feel Later—What is common to job loss, career loss, and business loss? They all involve coping with difficult emotions, all likely tap into important survival needs, and they all demand you create a new normal.

What is radically different with these types of losses from the losses we considered earlier is they seldom allow you the luxury of taking time to cope with your emotions. Most people need to replace their lost income—fast. Job hunting demands you present only the most positive emotions and confident attitude, at a time when you may feel neither. If you have a family who depends on you, you likely are in the position of reassuring them when it would be nice if someone reassured you.

Don't be surprised if emotions that necessity required you to ignore come knocking at your door later. They tend to show up only when you feel safe again—safe in your life and safe in your emotions. These were the feelings you had to keep at bay because you had bills to pay and food to buy at the same time you had to find a new job. When the emotions arrive, recognize the fact you can allow them now is validation that you have moved forward in a positive direction. You are no longer in survival mode.

Loss through Aging

Remember when all you ever wanted was to be 18 years old? Then, poof, you were. You blew out the last candles on your cake and announced to your parents, "Now I can do what I want—I'm 18!" Then you asked for the keys to their car and some gas money from their wallets and permission to stay out late with your friends to celebrate. Losing the teenage fantasy of adulthood was just the first of a long list of losses to come.

At first it's subtle, then it gets louder, and then it roars. In the beginning, many of the losses of aging are really losses of innocence. To master riding that shiny new bike you learned you must fall down—and get back up. You only get one first love, typically followed by a first heartbreak. You may be certain you will never survive, but then you do.

Before you know it, adolescence is in the rear view mirror and you are a young adult. You work diligently to create the life of your dreams and desires. You develop relationships, start a family, and launch your career. You are young and strong and full of energy! You are making decisions that will affect you for the rest of your life, for better and for worse.

Every YES decision you make means you said NO to something else. Choose to forego your career to stay home with a young family? You pay the price in years unavailable to grow your career, never really knowing for certain what those missed opportunities were. Choose to forego a family now in favor of growing your career? You forfeit the opportunity and perks of being a young parent, or maybe you wait so long you lose the option of ever being a biological parent at all.

Blink your eyes and midlife arrives. Midlife transitions are very real and love to grab our attention around significant birthdays. A mid-life crisis is an option but not a necessity.

Mid-life is a key time for doing a major life review. This is when people compare goals and expectations to see how closely the two match, and make adjustments if they don't. This is frequently a life stage when marriages must be re-born or often end, friendships are re-evaluated, old careers may be shed and new ones initiated. Mid-life can be a powerful time of profound change.

Here it comes—the Big Five OH! All the things you got away with physically in your younger days show up demanding payment. That high school football injury refuses to leave you alone. All that sun worshipping you did in college in your cute little bikini has you shopping for wrinkle cream and a good dermatologist. You start buying hormones at the drug store instead of making them effortlessly on your own. A night of passion may include the help of little blue pills you see marketed on television by silver haired actors pretending to be romantic. Maybe you find your nest is now empty—a major change even if it is a welcome one and a difficult one if it is not.

Here come the "Golden Years." You don't know how they arrived so fast, but they do. You mock the person who came up with the term. You look in the mirror and don't recognize the person looking back. Your body doesn't let you do what you want to do, let alone all the things you used to do. You have said good-bye to too many loved ones, and may even strangely find yourself getting used to it.

Loss of Health

Loss of health through illness or injury is probably the most humbling experience a person can have. Even the strongest of the strong can find themselves dependent on others for their most basic needs. If you are a person who has always valued having control in your life, finding out how little control you really have can be more than sobering.

Living with physical pain may be the ultimate challenge, especially when the condition is chronic, no real end in sight. It forces you to make difficult decisions about medications that may help at best and bring miserable side effects at worst. You may never have had a problem with depression before but with chronic pain find yourself battling it now. You may be frustrated with your medical care and the healthcare system, just when you need them most.

I Surrender!

Does all this loss seem just too overwhelming, even discouraging? It depends on how you look at it. When you realize loss has always been part of your life, each moment different from the last and the next, it may not seem quite so daunting. The more we embrace this truth, the less we try to control it, the freer we are to live our lives with less fear and greater acceptance.

What Do I Do?

- *Give yourself credit for all the things you already know about grief and loss.* Understand that new losses create new experiences and a need for new awareness. Learning is a life-long process.
- *Take the path of least resistance.* The less you fight, the more you accept your situation and your emotions, the smoother your journey will be. Make peace with loss.
- *Find or create something to look forward to every day.* No matter how insignificant, make sure that when you wake up tomorrow there is something you can get excited about. It can be a movie you've been waiting to see, lunch with a friend, writing a fresh version of your resume, starting a new class or learning a new skill. The possibilities are endless. Find what works for you.
- *Know you always have choices.* You may feel trapped, but you always have options. You can choose how you feel, how you react, and how you handle adversity. What is one thing you can do right now to change your present reality into a new one? Just your thoughts have the power to change your situation, not to mention your actions.
- *If forgiveness is needed, start first by forgiving yourself.* For many, this is the most difficult task of all. Often people are surprised when they realize how harshly they judge themselves. Hindsight too often includes regrets for deeds

done or not done, for words uttered or never said. You will never know what might have happened had your situation been different, but you do know being hard on yourself doesn't make a difficult situation any better.

- *Forgive others when you are ready.* People often shame themselves into forgiveness, believing they "should" forgive, or feeling guilty because they can't forgive. Real forgiveness can require hard work and time. Forgive when you are genuinely willing and able to forgive from your heart, and not a minute sooner.

- *Know genuine forgiveness is about freedom.* Forgiving someone does not mean you have a new best friend. It doesn't even mean you have to talk with the person or make amends. Forgiveness means you release obsessive thoughts about the individual who hurt you. There is no longer a desire to get even, punish, or think about what you wish you had said or done differently, in fact you may no longer think of them at all. Forgiving means you have put the past where it belongs and can head toward your future unencumbered. Forgiveness is something you do for yourself.

- *Live today with passion and gratitude.* Tomorrow can only give you hope and direction while yesterday provides memories and lessons. Today gives you an amazing grand buffet of endless possibilities. Choose wisely because the choices you make today become the reality of your tomorrow.

※

Talking about grief and loss experiences, obtaining valuable new information, getting answers to tough questions often stirs up a whole new set of questions. We've covered a lot of material so far, but we're not done yet. Next we look at questions you may still have that have not yet been answered.

Chapter 8

Questions Answered and Myths Dispelled

Just as the subject of grief and loss is endless, so are the questions that go with it. This chapter addresses some of the most commonly asked questions grieving people bring to therapy in their search for answers, clarification, and peace of mind.

Question: Am I crazy?

Answer: If you weren't crazy before your loss, you probably aren't crazy after—you just feel like it. Dial the phone and forget who you're calling? Drive down the road and no clue where you are going? Find a bottle of shampoo in the fridge—twice? That's typical grief behavior.

Most newly bereaved people find themselves confused by their own behaviors in the early days of grief. It's like you don't even know yourself anymore. You wonder if you have lost your mind, but more importantly, you wonder if you will ever get it back.

Your brain is working overtime to assimilate the changes coming at you faster than you can process. It's as if you are taking a tennis lesson and the ball machine goes haywire, slinging so many balls at you so fast that all you can do is duck. Your body is physically depleted and your mind is on overload, even the simplest tasks become difficult. This immediate after effect will pass, but there are things you can do to help yourself make the process a little easier.

Caring for yourself, even if you don't feel like it, is the first line of defense. Get some rest, however and wherever you can. Eat some nourishing food while avoiding sugary desserts that give you a short mood boost, only to leave you feeling worse all too soon. Get some exercise—even just a short walk in fresh air can calm some of the noisiest of heads. Taking care of yourself as your top priority will help you regain your focus as quickly as possible, and it goes a long way in helping you face the difficult days ahead.

Question: What is the fastest way to get through all these painful emotions?

Answer: There is no fast, quick or easy way. The best way through it is to do it. Let how you feel be your gauge rather than the days on a calendar. Know that it is not just okay to experience your emotions, it is healthy and it is normal. Your heart knows how to grieve, even if your mind is reeling. Trust your body to show you the way.

Practice checking in with yourself often by frequently asking, "What do I need right now?" If the answer is, "I need rest," then rest. If the answer is, "I need to be alone," be alone. If the answer is, "I need to be around my loved ones," go find them. Start with these little questions in the beginning and tackle the big questions only when you must and when you can.

Question: It's been two weeks; shouldn't I be over it by now?

Answer: The reality of your loss may just be starting to sink in at two weeks. Expecting yourself to be "over it" is unrealistic and may make you feel even worse than you already feel. Expect the first year to be the most difficult as you work to create a new normal, and consider removing the term "over it" from your vocabulary. If others around you use the term, ignore them.

Question: Is there something wrong with me if I don't express my emotions openly?

Answer: Keeping your emotions and expression of them private is simply one way of coping that is neither right nor wrong. Grief expressed in private is just as valid as grief expressed in public.

Question: Should I take medication to help me cope with the strain and pressure caused by my loss?

Answer: Some people avoid medications or any type of mind-altering substances when they are grieving, choosing to feel the full range of their emotions without interference. They are not being brave, and they are not being foolish, they are simply grieving people making the choice they feel is right for them.

Choosing to see your physician for short term medications to help manage your initial reactions to your loss is another option. This is a very personal choice with no one right or wrong solution. If you do choose to use medication, be careful to keep in mind how easy it is to make mistakes or feel confused when you are in the initials throws of grief. It would be easy to forget if you took a pill and accidentally took two or forgot to take an important medication at all. This might be a good time to ask a family member for help or temporarily use a daily pill dispenser box to help you keep on track.

Make sure you understand what medication you will be taking, the correct dose and when to take it. Know the potential side affects you may experience and how they could hurt as well as help. Ask your doctor how long you should take the medication, what you should do if you experience any adverse reactions, and be sure to check for interactions with any other medications you may be taking. Pharmacists can also be a good resource to answer your questions and guide you in the right direction.

If you have been diagnosed previously with some type of mental health condition and use medication regularly to help manage your symptoms, the extreme stress of grieving may require a re-evaluation. If at all possible, see the same medical provider who treated you before your loss, someone who knows you and your history so an accurate assessment can be made. Be sure to advise your doctor that you are grieving a significant loss as this can affect your physical as well as your emotional well being.

Question: They say "time heals all wounds." Can't I just wait it out?

Answer: Time alone does not heal all wounds. Even a painful cut on your finger that appears to magically disappear actually goes through a healing process from the painful cut to the scar that remains. What the passage of time does offer is the ability to absorb and assimilate your loss and the chance to rest a weary mind, body and heart.

Question: I can't stop crying. What's wrong with me?

Answer: In the early days following a painful loss, it may seem like you will never stop crying. Grieving people often say they are afraid if they start crying they will never be able to stop. As powerful as the feelings may be, the reality does not support the theory. Have you ever heard of someone crying for years without stopping?

Grief can be a strange thing. You can be sobbing and choking to breathe one minute, then all of a sudden feel kind of hungry the next. The quick change may even startle you, leaving you once again wondering if you really are losing your mind. In fact, this is your body's built-in self protection early warning system telling you, "That's enough for now." Let your inner wisdom guide you on this difficult journey.

Question: I haven't cried at all. What's wrong with me?

Answer: You are just as normal in your grief as the person who feels they can't stop crying. You may be in shock. You may be so overwhelmed you are doing your best to simply function. Not crying doesn't mean you are strong and it does not mean you are weak. There is no standard for the correct number of tears.

Question: *How will I know if I need professional help?*

Answer: There is a difference between needing and wanting to get professional help. If several weeks have passed and you find you are unable to resume simple tasks and routines, a visit to a qualified mental health provider is in line. On the other hand, if you simply feel the need to talk with someone outside of your grief community, someone who is objective and supportive and refrains from judgement, then you may find talking with a professional experienced in grief work very beneficial.

If you are looking for a therapist skilled in grief and loss work, start by asking those around you if there is someone they can recommend. If you are shopping from a list of unknown providers, begin by calling and asking for a brief phone interview in order to get a first impression to help you make your selection. Be sure you find a licensed professional. A license is designed to protect the public by proving the clinician has completed minimum required training, testing, internships, and participates in ongoing education. Any licensed professional should be happy to share their credentials with you, and the physical license should be posted in the therapy office where it is easily seen.

If you see a therapist who cannot contain his or her own emotions when hearing about your loss, or you feel the need to take care of the therapist's feelings, find another therapist. The job of a therapist is not to join you in your pain and sadness, but to listen with compassion and provide witness to your story and your experience. Find the right person for you and don't be afraid to ask for what you need.

Question: *Talking about it only makes me feel worse. Why shouldn't I just push my thoughts and feelings aside and get on with my life?*

Answer: Staying busy and not dwelling on your grief can be an option, and it can be helpful at times. However, staying busy to avoid your grief does not mean you are getting on with your life.

Rejecting your thoughts and feelings does not mean they are not still there; it just means they are operating under the surface and away from conscious awareness. Think about a computer virus that is corrupting your system without you even knowing. Even if you can't see it, the virus is still there. The longer it takes for you to find it the more damage it does and the harder it is to clean up.

Question: If I take my focus off my loved one's death, our final hours together, I'm afraid I will lose the only connection I have left. What's wrong with holding onto my grief?

Answer: It's actually the other way around. When you stay focused on death, you cannot be focused on the bigger story—life. When you stay locked in your grief, you deny yourself any feelings of joy from memories of happier times. And when you hold onto your pain, it means every time you think of the person you lost your pain is renewed.

Letting go of the person's death does not mean you are letting go of the person. Letting go of the death allows you to celebrate their entire life, cherish the time you had together, and bring your loved one back into your life in a whole new way through the many memories you shared. They may be physically gone from your life, but in this way they can very much live on in your heart for the rest of your days.

Question: I thought I was doing okay but now I'm worse. Am I having a grief relapse?

Answer: Grief is not an illness or an addiction, conditions where recovery may include relapses. Grief is an emotion. It comes in waves—sometimes a lot and sometimes a little. The feelings will pass, and the feelings will likely return multiple times—both are normal in the grief process. You may be okay, but you may also still be grieving—possibly at the same time.

Question: What is the difference between grieving and mourning?

Answer: Grieving means you are experiencing the feelings of grief, such as distress, suffering and sorrow. Mourning is the physical act of grieving, the outward signs of grief as in wearing black clothes or an arm band or veil. Acts of mourning are born out of cultural beliefs and practices, often varying from one culture to the next.

Question: Is it true there is no right or wrong way to grieve?

Answer: Grief is a feeling and there is no right or wrong way to feel. Grief is only one of many emotions including happy, sad, angry, and glad. We certainly enjoy some feelings over others, but they are all nothing more and nothing less than feelings that come and go over the course of time.

Unlike grief, however, there can be healthy and unhealthy ways to express feelings, unhealthy ways to mourn or behave. Abusing drugs and/or alcohol to medicate or numb difficult emotions is unhealthy and risky behavior. Raging at drivers in other vehicles to avoid facing your own anger is unhealthy and risky behavior.

Rage and anger are not synonyms, not at all the same thing. Anger is a normal, healthy, human emotion, something we all experience. Rage is not a normal, healthy, human emotion. Rage is anger infected, out of control and harmful. Rage is when people and things get hurt and broken through actions, words and deeds. If you find yourself raging, your actions and emotions out of control beyond the initial period following your loss, it may be time for professional intervention.

Question: Is it normal to be angry with the person who died for leaving you? If I'm not angry, does it mean I am in denial?

Answer: You absolutely do not have to be angry with your loved one for dying, but you might be angry with your loved one for dying. It's possible to even be grateful for a loved one's death, not because you are glad they died but because you are glad they are released from suffering. Wanting what is best for another person, even if it brings you pain, is genuine love.

Question: I feel guilty when I laugh. How will I know when it's okay to laugh again? Will it ever be okay to laugh again?

Answer: Just as crying is "okay," so is laughing. You may even find yourself doing them both at the same time. You might be startled the first time a real laugh escapes your mouth, perhaps shocked it's even possible amidst so many dark emotions. Embrace laughter. Share your funny stories of your loved one and let everyone join in. We heal through both laughter and tears.

Question: I have grieved the loss of people close to me who have died, but I am beyond devastated by the loss of my pet. Is there something wrong with me that my pet dying is having a greater impact on me than when people in my life have died?

Answer: Believe it or not, this is a commonly asked question in grief and loss counseling. For those of us who love our animals and consider them part of our families, the loss of a pet can be truly devastating. Rather than trying to rank which death is more significant, consider the impact of your loss on your every day life.

Your pet gave you constant unconditional love in a way no human ever can or will. You shared frequent physical contact and affection, including on days when you never left the house or interacted with another human. You were greeted at the door each time you walked in as if you were the Grand Ruler of the World. When they are gone, we are constantly reminded of how their absence permeates our lives from morning to night, from bedroom to kitchen to patio. How could we not miss them?

If you are not an animal lover and are reading this in an effort to understand someone you love who is grieving the loss of a pet, here is the truth: You don't have to understand. No one ever completely understands another person's loss. Just listen and be supportive, and above all else, do not try to fix the problem. It isn't a problem; it is grief.

Question: My friend who I care very much about is grieving deeply for the loss of a close loved one. What can I do to help my friend?

Answer: First, stop talking and start listening. Second, don't worry about saying something brilliant or saying the right thing, just keep listening. Forget the silly almost obligatory phrase, "Let me know if there's anything I can do." Just do something! Go wash their dishes. Take their dirty laundry, deliver it back clean, and don't worry if they even noticed. Pick up their kids from school, feed them, make sure they do their homework, and deliver them home bathed in their pajamas. With words, less is more. With actions, more is more.

Chapter 9

Helplessness to Resilience—
The Author's Story

The Background

I spent nearly two decades climbing the Fortune 500 corporate ladder as a Human Resources professional. Achieving impressive titles, corner offices, and a salary in the top 3 percent earning bracket for women in the United States, by most people's standards, I was successful.

I enjoyed my work, and as a single parent I appreciated the financial security it provided for my family. There was never a moment to think about the effects of my choices—there was only one direction and that was straight ahead.

You don't notice when "Golden Handcuffs" are slipped onto your wrists. These are the increasing perks you get that make leaving an employer foolish at first, and nearly impossible later and on your terms. At some point you realize they are there, but you not only like them, you want more. Then, you start to realize doors are closing on other opportunities, and those shiny invisible bracelets begin to get a little tighter and a little less shiny. Still, you don't really pay much attention to your "Golden Handcuffs" until they cut, you begin to bleed, and you start to feel trapped.

Disillusionment began to set in for me as the further my career advanced, the less personal satisfaction I got from the work I was doing. I lived on airplanes, sat in tedious meetings, slept in hotel beds more often than my own, and jumped through one political hoop after another. I found my own integrity out of sync too many times, and that created inner turmoil I could not effectively ignore.

I knew for a long time that some day I wanted and needed to be self employed. I also couldn't help but notice in my early 40's there were few co-workers over 55 to be found. I'd have been a fool not to know some day it would be my turn, and I began envisioning my future independence long before it was ever a real option.

When my sons became emancipated young adults, I found myself with a new sense of freedom. For the first time, I could take real risks. If things went poorly I would harm no one but myself, and I did a crazy thing. I accepted an assignment to open a large Southwest business operating out of Las Vegas. This was going to be fun, and fun was something I definitely needed to add to my life! Or, at least, that was the plan.

Everything that could go wrong quickly went very wrong. It started with a massive earthquake in California that damaged the profitability of the business, and it all went downhill from there. The business never had a chance and the future was easy to predict. Management heads were rolling every direction. It was time to make another change, and fast.

I aggressively launched my next job search. In no time, I connected with my dream job and it looked like I was headed back east for my next corporate gig. I should have been excited, but I was tired of moving, I was travel weary, and I was sick of making friends I had to leave. I had fallen in love with the desert and wanted badly to stay, but there really seemed to be no choice to stay. Little did I know the change headed my way or just how mistaken I could be.

From Helplessness

The obnoxious phone jarred me awake too early on the morning of December 24, 1994. I figured it had to be someone calling from the Eastern Time Zone because it happened so often and was always annoying. I remember swearing to myself when I moved back to the east I would never be so inconsiderate of Pacific Time Zone people again.

The call was from an Ohio relative letting me know she had received a call from a local hospital. She said my mother had been taken there by ambulance, but she had no idea why. Hospital? Ambulance?

I was baffled. I'd spoken with Mom on the phone the previous evening. She had taken the day off work to finish last-minute Christmas shopping and said she didn't feel well. Her back had been bothering her and treatment had not relieved the discomfort, but there were no other apparent issues with her health. We were both tired from holiday stress and agreed to get some rest. I promised to check on her in the morning, and we said, "Good-night." I couldn't even guess how she could be in the hospital, via ambulance no less, only hours later.

I quickly called long distance to the hospital, expecting to get a volunteer giving me some generic status report. Instead, I was immediately connected to the attending physician. What on earth was happening?

The physician was kind, but direct and to the point. She informed me my mother had called for an ambulance, let the Emergency Medical Technicians into her home, and proceeded to have a massive heart attack. She said they "lost her" in the ambulance on the way to the hospital, succeeded in reviving her, and she'd had a second attack that had destroyed the main valve in her heart. She told me my mother was not going to live.

Well, that was just absurd. This had to be some awful mistake. I just talked to Mom and, except for the back ache, she was fine. My mother was young, only 69 years old, and came from a long line of strong women who live and lived forever. She'd never even been in the hospital, other than to give birth decades before. Her own mother lived to be 106! I was taking the situation seriously, but clearly the physician had to be horribly mistaken.

Being the dutiful daughter who loved her mother very much, I was faced with my first choice. If there was any truth to what I was being told, I needed to be my mother's voice and advocate as I had promised to do. Would I honor her wishes made so clear to me in the past, or would I choose what I wanted which was not to lose my mother? In my mind, there was no choice as I said, "My mother did not want any heroic measures ever taken on her behalf. I do not want her to be placed on life support." There, I said it.

Ignorance isn't always bliss. Without hesitation, the physician informed me that not only was my mother already on life support, but that if it was disconnected, she would immediately die. I was then slapped with my next choice when she asked, "What do you want?"

What do I want? What do I want! I want to go to the bathroom since I was just so rudely jerked awake. I want some caffeine, a whole vat of caffeine! I want to go back to sleep and end this awful nightmare, wake up and start this day over again. This was not happening.

As calmly as I could, I told the physician to do whatever tests she needed to do so we could make a fully-informed decision. I told her while she completed all the tests, I would be on an airplane to get there as fast as I could, and allow the family time to gather. She agreed but followed with the warning, "Don't expect your mom to be alive when you get here." This woman sure wasn't cutting me any slack. I'd say I was speechless, but I told her the only thing I knew to say, the only thing I knew to be true. "She'll wait for me."

I went into achievement-oriented auto pilot. Shock really does come in handy sometimes. I made arrangements to vanish instantly with no idea when I would return. I slung clothes into a suitcase and froze when the next choice gave me a sour look at my situation. Did I pack an outfit appropriate for a funeral, my mother's funeral? Knowing the one thing my mother was most proud of in her entire life was her children, I made my wardrobe choice for her. I packed an outfit I was to wear only one more time.

I won't attempt to describe the flight from Vegas to Cleveland; I'm not sure I could. Nothing was real. I got into my rental car and somehow an hour later walked into the hospital just before midnight.

I had no idea what to expect. It was so hushed, so quiet. There were Christmas decorations everywhere. I tiptoed into the Coronary Care Unit and was amazed when I was happily greeted by multiple medical people calling me by name, saying they knew I'd just flown in from Las Vegas, talking as if they'd known me forever. My mother was alive! They took me into see her, and there were those big brown eyes that just sparkled the minute she saw me. My mother waited for me.

I visited for only the few minutes allowed and left the hospital to head for my home away from home, my aunt and uncle's house. Amazingly, driving through a city I was born, raised and lived in for 30 years, I got lost, really lost. I'm still not sure exactly how I finally arrived at my destination.

Christmas Day was spent with family, short visits in and out with Mom who actually seemed to be doing better. The staff was encouraging as the day went on, in my mind confirming my gene pool theory as fact—we are strong women who live forever. We got the encouraging news that Mom would be moved out of CCU to a regular room in the morning. Feeling hopeful and a little more relaxed, we all realized how hungry and exhausted we were and went to enjoy a late holiday feast while Mom rested.

Then, it happened again. I had barely fallen asleep, complete with a too full stomach, when the hateful ring of the phone woke the household in the very early morning hours of December 26. It was the hospital. They said, "Come now."

Some day I may forgive my uncle for driving so slow, for his determination to get us to the hospital safely on snowy roads. Half way there, I knew it no longer mattered. I knew the moment my mother was gone.

I jumped out of the car before it stopped in the hospital parking lot and I ran. The elevator doors opened for me almost as if by magic, the staff was waiting for me as I walked off. They shared the news that was not news. They said things I didn't understand, things that really didn't matter anymore, anyway. Their words were a garbled mess and all I could do was nod my head, indicating I understood when I didn't understand at all.

I walked into the room alone. There were those same brown eyes but no flash, no reaction to my arrival, no reaction to anything at all. I knew I should close them, but I just couldn't do it. I touched her arm that was cool but still warm at the same time. It was immediately clear to me--this was not my mother. This was my mother's body. It looked so small. I didn't know it was possible to hurt so much, or how I could go on if it didn't stop. I didn't think I would ever be able to breathe again.

I am fortunate to look like my mother, but in that moment the similarity brought anything but comfort. I was seeing my own death on top of my mother's. I realized how little time I really have left, and how precious every minute really is. My own life review flew through my mind with clarity I had never experienced before, and my new normal began to form. I vowed in that moment to experience every single emotion in honor of my amazing mother and this tremendous loss. Then I left the room to go throw up.

After the funeral and the obligatory dinner, I went back into the desperately-needed safety of my aunt and uncle's home. I needed to just sit in a chair and do nothing. But, another surprise was waiting for me when I arrived instead. There it was—an overnight package straight from Corporate America, MY Corporate America. Inside the package was a stack of papers with a note from my boss on top. He wanted to know if I'd be able to get my report done and submitted on time.

I would say that this was my next big choice, but in all honesty, I think the choice made itself. I got the report done and in on time, and I began creating my exit strategy.

I withdrew from the new job opportunity. I applied and was accepted into graduate school. Seven months later, I left my job, and I left my corporate career and life. I planted roots in the desert where some amazing things grow when you least expect it.

To Resilience

I have never once regretted my decisions that led me to this day. I tore through graduate school in record time. I served internships in simple little community clinics, so different from where I'd been. It was so much fun to be learning again! I was doing the work that I loved in a setting that mattered and with people determined to make a better life for themselves.

It will come as no surprise that I began to work with grief and loss cases early in my new career, or that I never stopped. I launched my solo private practice in 1998, and I love my work as much or more today as I did then. Today, I define what success means to me instead of allowing others to do it for me. Today, the definition of success starts with happiness. Today, I am successful.

I still miss my mom all these years later. I have never completely run out of tears, but I did work through the pain, and I did breathe again. The sadness slowly faded and was replaced with an acceptance that allows me to have her with me always. Never a big fan of therapy, I wonder what she would think of her daughter, the psychotherapist. I wonder what she would say about her six amazing adult grandchildren or her adorable six little great grandchildren.

Not surprisingly, there have been more losses in my life along the way--each unique, each devastating in it's own right. My most recent loss was literally as I was writing Chapter 4 of this book. I was sitting at the kitchen table, writing some notes late on a Sunday, when I had to rush my 8-year-old Terrier to the animal hospital. She was fine and three weeks later cancer took her from me, and the world lost the best therapy dog ever. It seems there should be a limit as to how much sadness one heart can hold, but I haven't found what that limit is.

Once again born out of pain, I found myself faced with another difficult choice. Feeling saturated with loss, part of me wanted to just "delete" this whole manuscript and never talk about it again. Ironically or intuitively, I'd been stuck for weeks unable to write a decent version of the section on pet loss. I came home without my girl, I sat down alone and we wrote the piece together in a matter of minutes. I knew I had to keep writing and I've never stopped.

I miss each of my loved ones I have lost so very much. I do not hesitate to say that a part of me I will never get back went with every one of them. But, a part of them I cherish and hold closely in my heart has stayed with me as well, and I will never let go. Whether I shared DNA with those I have lost or not, this was and is my family. My life has been richer because of the family I was given and the family I have chosen. I wouldn't want it any other way.

Conclusion

What you have just read was a whole lot of information crammed into a very little book. The goals were to help you understand at least one thing you didn't understand before, to lighten your pain even just the slightest, and to do both as quickly as possible.

We needed to cover as much territory as we could in as little time as possible. The text needed to be pragmatic, straight forward, honest, and user-friendly for people looking for and needing answers NOW. The challenge was to address the universal experience of loss at the same time respect the unique experience of each reader. And it needed to deeply honor the very personal experiences of the people whose stories were shared.

Armed with a custom road map on how to create a new normal, your new normal, hopefully you now have a sense of direction. Each step may not be clear, but you will figure them out as you go. You have proven tools available to you to help you along the way, tools that have worked for other grieving people who have survived their losses. You now know how to separate fact from fiction.

Today you vow to trust yourself to know what is best for you first, and listen to others second, including all the things you read in this book. Take what works and pitch what doesn't. You are the boss, the expert on your loss. Acknowledge that grief and loss have always been a part of your life, so learning to live with them not only makes sense, it is necessary and smart.

Now you know you aren't stuck or trapped or out of options. You have choices. You have many choices. The question is what will you do with them, starting today, starting now?

CPSIA information can be obtained
at www.ICGtesting.com
Printed in the USA
FSHW02n1003220918
52472FS